Double Feature

John Logan

methuen | drama

LONDON • NEW YORK • OXFORD • NEW DELHI • SYDNEY

METHUEN DRAMA
Bloomsbury Publishing Plc
50 Bedford Square, London, WC1B 3DP, UK
1385 Broadway, New York, NY 10018, USA
29 Earlsfort Terrace, Dublin 2, Ireland

BLOOMSBURY, METHUEN DRAMA and the Methuen
Drama logo are trademarks of Bloomsbury Publishing Plc

First published in Great Britain 2024

Copyright © John Logan, 2024

John Logan has asserted his right under the Copyright, Designs
and Patents Act, 1988, to be identified as author of this work.

Cover design by SWD Design

Cover image: Tippi Hedren and Alfred Hitchcock
at Cannes © Bettmann / Getty Images

A catalogue record for this book is available from the British Library.

A catalog record for this book is available from the Library of Congress.

ISBN: PB: 978-1-3504-7164-1
ePDF: 978-1-3504-7166-5
eBook: 978-1-3504-7165-8

Series: Modern Plays

Typeset by Mark Heslington Ltd, Scarborough, North Yorkshire

To find out more about our authors and books visit
www.bloomsbury.com and sign up for our newsletters.

Double Feature was first performed at Hampstead Theatre, London on 8 February 2024. The cast was as follows:

Vincent Price	**Jonathan Hyde**
Alfred Hitchcock	**Ian McNeice**
Michael Reeves	**Rowan Polonski**
Tippi Hedren	**Joanna Vanderham**

Writer	John Logan
Director	Jonathan Kent
Designer	Anthony Ward
Lighting	Hugh Vanstone
Sound	Paul Groothuis
Casting	Sarah Bird CDG

We are grateful to Heather Acton & Peter Williams for kindly supporting the production.

Double Feature

In 1962–63, Alfred Hitchcock directed Tippi Hedren in *The Birds*. The following year he directed her in *Marnie* . . . They never worked together again.

In 1967, Michael Reeves directed Vincent Price in *Witchfinder General* . . . They were planning on doing another film the following year, but Reeves died of a barbiturate overdose.

Characters (*in order of appearance*)

Vincent Price, *American actor. Fifty-six years old.*
Michael Reeves, *British film director. Twenty-four years old.*
Tippi Hedren, *American actress. Thirty-four years old.*
Alfred Hitchcock, *British film director. Sixty-four years old.*

Setting

Michael Reeves' rented cottage in Bury St Edmunds, Suffolk . . . November, 1967.

Alfred Hitchcock's bungalow on the Universal lot, Los Angeles . . . March, 1964.

Set

Both stories share one set simultaneously.

Reeves' rented cottage and Hitchcock's spacious bungalow are both done in an English country style: Reeves' cottage because it is actually in the English countryside; Hitchcock's because his art directors and designers have perfectly recreated it in Los Angeles.

There is a kitchen area. A dining table area filled with books, scripts, notes, and storyboards. The living room has a sofa and a bar area. There are a few imitation Staffordshire china dogs here and there. A print of Turner's painting "Rain, Steam, and Speed—The Great Western Railway" hangs on a wall.

This play should be performed without an intermission.

Spacious living room and kitchen area in an English country style.

Night.

There's a door to the hallway to the outside, and another entrance into the bedroom and rest of the house.

Doorbell rings . . . Nothing . . . Doorbell rings again.

The sound of the front door opening and closing.

Vincent Price *enters from outside. He's tall and imposing. He wears a fedora and a gorgeous velvet jacket under his overcoat. Naturally theatrical and with a deliciously ribald sense of humor, he knows his own worth and is wise to the ways of the world . . . He loves being* **Vincent Price**.

Tonight though, he is at the end of his rope.

Looks around.

Nothing.

He goes to the kitchen area and checks inside the stove . . . Hmm . . . Not pleased with what's cooking.

Looks around again.

Vincent (*calls*)   Where's the goddamn boy genius?

Michael Reeves *enters from the other part of the house. He's young and lean, wears a dark turtleneck and dark trousers. Slip-on shoes without socks. He's intense and driven; neurotic of passion, melancholy of spirit. Not particularly comfortable around people. Speaks with a posh accent that embarrasses him; he comes from money.*

Occasionally his hands shake from tension.

And he's anxious tonight . . . He chatters nervously:

Reeves   God, God, sorry. Is it raining again? That'll slow us down tomorrow. But it'll look good on camera. I never understand why directors avoid the weather. Weather's *real*. People understand weather. It's a shared experience and brings the audience into the film, doesn't it? Let me take your—

Vincent *has tossed his hat and overcoat on a piece of furniture.*

Reeves   Ah, good. Make yourself at home. You've not been here I think. Nice place they found for me. Hardly need all the space but, well, here we are. Let me get you a—

Vincent *has already moved to the bar area; pours himself a large drink.*

Reeves   Ah, good, good. Maybe I'll have one. No, no. Have to cook yet. And shoot tomorrow of course. Early day for us both, so we best—

Vincent   Michael.

Reeves *stops.*

Vincent   Who do I have to fuck to get off this picture?

Reeves   Ha!

Vincent *stares at him . . . gimlet-eyed . . . takes a slow sip. Waits.*

Reeves   All right, about what happened today—I lost my temper. I'm sorry.

Vincent (*icy calm*)   You derided me in front of the entire cast and crew. At considerable length, Mr. Reeves.

Reeves   Look, Vincent, Vinnie, Vincent . . . I know it hasn't been easy for us, there's no use pretending. I'm thoroughly ashamed about today. I was a bloody ass and I'll make it up to you—it's just—there's so much pressure and . . . (*He notices his hands are shaking and conceals them.*) . . . there's no money to make the film and no time—and I'm trying to make something decent—*we're* trying to make something decent—so I'm afraid graciousness has been left behind— especially today. It's all down to me and I'm sorry.

Vincent   Please. Why don't you leave the face-pulling to the professionals?

Reeves   I've apologized, so let's forget it and move on. Agreed?

He offers his hand. **Vincent** *does not take it.*

Vincent   No, sirree. No, no. Not this time, Michael. Not *again*, Michael. . . . After the *public humiliation* you visited upon me today, I retired to my trailer and made a phone call. Just one. 'Twas to Los Angeles. 'Twas to my redoubtable agents. They assured me of my legal standing and therefore, Mr. Reeves, I am hereby informing you that I'm exercising Clause 17, Paragraph 5 in my contract.

Reeves   Clause 17?

Vincent   Allowing me to leave the picture due to irreconcilable personal differences with the director.

Reeves   Leave the picture . . .

Vincent   That's right, Michael. Adios and good luck.

Reeves   For heaven's sake, you can't walk off the film!

Vincent   Watch me, kiddo.

Reeves   But—but—that'll kill it. All the work, everyone's work, my work, my film, my career, my—goddamn it! You're being absurd now! You're being fucking absurd and fucking selfish, stop it immediately!

Vincent   There's the Michael Reeves I know. What did it take? Two minutes?

Reeves   What do you expect me to do? Do you expect me to beg?

Vincent   Yes. I expect you to beg. I expect you to humiliate yourself, as you've been humiliating me for the past three weeks. Every indignity you've heaped on me—in front of the crew and my fellow actors—I expect you to make amends for right now. You will fail, because you are incapable of a genuine human interaction that's not storyboarded, so I'll leave tomorrow and return to sun-kissed Santa Monica and your movie will never get finished—and the studio won't raise a finger because I'm their goddamn Edgar Allan Poe fucking top-of-the-bill headliner and worth more to them than any upstart, counter-jumping, hippie-mod, twenty-four-year-old *auteur* with delusions of Truffaut swimming in his self-important imagination . . . So . . . yes . . . my dear boy . . . Beg.

Reeves *glares at him.*

But the stakes are high.

He swallows, begs.

Reeves   Vincent . . . Sincerely . . . From the bottom of my heart I—

Vincent   On your knees.

Beat.

Your knees are those things between your cock and your feet.

Reeves   You've got to be kidding.

Beat.

Fuck yourself.

Beat.

Go on, leave the film, go back to America, you old side of ham, you irredeemable eye-rolling, smirking fake of a jobbing hack actor. I'll get Donald Pleasence like I wanted in the first place and we'll reshoot your scenes without the fucking camp thank you very much!

Beat.

But then he kneels.

Beat.

Vincent *walks to him . . . right to him . . . stands close . . . crotch to face.*

Looks down at him.

Beat.

Reeves   Please. Just stay for dinner. Give me a chance . . .
I'll do anything.

Vincent   Really? It means that much?

Reeves   . . . Yes.

Vincent *looks down at him. Reaches down and takes* **Reeves**' *face. Leans very close. Close enough to kiss him.*

Suspense . . . What will **Vincent** *do?*

He whispers.

Vincent   How does it feel? Being degraded.

Reeves *does not answer.*

Vincent *stands briskly, rubs his hands, and moves to the kitchen area.*

Vincent   Now get up and tell me what's for dinner!

Reeves *stands, a little shaken by the encounter.*

Vincent   I glanced in but the smell was so villainous I risked no more.

Reeves *removes a pan with fish from the oven. They examine it.*

Reeves   Um. It's—ah—it's bream I think, I just asked the man at the counter. I don't really know much about cooking.

Vincent   Spectacularly so.

Reeves   I rang my mother and she told me to stick it in the pan with some butter and lemon. It's been roasting away on low; I was meant to baste it but I mean who can handle all that pressure?

He haphazardly flips and bastes the fish with the butter.

I've some water on for pasta too. Cook gave my mother this recipe because she said even a monkey could pull it off, which is pretty much me in the kitchen.

Vincent   Turner.

Reeves   I just did.

Vincent (*dry*)   The painting.

He moves to a print of Turner's "Rain, Steam, and Speed—The Great Western Railway" hanging on a wall.

Vincent   In all honesty, the only reason I'm still here is this print.

I thought to myself . . . any man who hangs a Turner can't be a complete cunt . . . (*He puts on his glasses and examines the print.*) . . . I buy art for Sears-Roebuck, so I'm always looking at pictures.

Reeves   You buy pictures for a department store?

Vincent   "The Vincent Price Collection." Bringing a little class to the benighted haciendas of greater suburbia . . . a flourish amidst the Tupperware and Astroturf.

Reeves   How do you choose which ones to buy?

Vincent   Hmm. End of the day, I buy the ones that make me feel something. Don't lecture me, don't prove to me how clever you are, don't be ironic—make me *feel*. Stop worrying that bream and come here.

Reeves *puts the fish back in the oven and joins* **Vincent**.

Vincent   Tell me what you see.

Reeves   Train coming along a bridge through the fog.

Vincent   Making you think of what?

Reeves (*quickly*)   *The Great Train Robbery. The General. Union Pacific. North by Northwest. Von Ryan's Express. Bridge on the River Kwai. Night Train to Munich. Strangers on a Train.*

Vincent   I could weep . . . Have you ever read a book?

Reeves   Not much for that.

Vincent   Ah, you're one of that new breed of Morlocks who live in the darkened movie theater, never seeing the light of day and losing all your natural pigmentation. Sometimes I wonder what new species will evolve from all you kids. What stunted, myopic cinema monsters you'll give rise to, and on what will you feed when all the celluloid dissolves into little pools of chemical goo? . . . Don't you think you might be missing something out there in the wide world of reality?

Reeves   Nothing that compares to film.

Vincent   What about music? Going to the theater?

Reeves   Theater makes me nervous. What if something goes wrong? What if they forget their lines? I can't stand that. The uncertainty makes me too anxious.

Vincent   It's too real for you.

Reeves   Oh, theater's not real, it's all painted faces and playing to the back balcony. Movies are real.

Vincent   Movies force you to look at things one way. That's not real. Some director and jobbing hack actors get together and film a scene. Once it's edited it never changes. *Et, voilà* . . . for all time there's the scene; set in stone, no options, no choices, no *ambiguity*. I repeat . . . that's not real. There's no *life*. It's immortal, yes, it'll last forever, but it's dead. Movies are the zombie art form.

Reeves   Paintings never change either. Are they zombies?

Vincent   Depends how you look at them . . . (*Re: the Turner.*) . . . You look at it like a movie fan—like a cinéaste hungry for plot and more plot—so you see one thing only . . . a train comes over a bridge.

Reeves   That's what it is.

Vincent   That's what it *shows*, that's not what it *is*.

With no warning, **Tippi Hedren** *enters from the hallway to the outside and crosses the stage.*

She's blonde and beautiful. She has a model's natural poise . . . she looks effortlessly composed and even posed. But beneath the outward grace, there's a staggering amount of inner strength.

She wears a chic grey Edith Head-style suit, gloves, and a pale green scarf.

She's dreading tonight.

Vincent *and* **Reeves** *do not see her.*

Vincent   All right then, Mr. Reeves. Shall we try to salvage your bream?

He chuckles, amused at himself, as he usually is . . . They move to the kitchen area, open some wine, and work on the fish.

Tippi   Hitch . . .?

Vincent   Did you pick the wine?

Reeves   Man at the shop recommended it. White with fish, yes?

Vincent   Only if you're bourgeois. Wine must suit the moment, not the dish.

Tippi   Hitch . . .?

Nothing.

Reeves *prepares a joint as* **Tippi** *prepares to light a cigarette.*

Her gloves make the task a little challenging but she doesn't take them off. She's about to light up . . . Sparks the lighter . . . But then stops . . . flame hovering before the cigarette . . .

She looks around again . . . her eyes scanning the room from place to place restlessly . . .

Suspenseful beat . . . What is she waiting for?

Vincent   But you must not let my culinary legerdemain distract you from my intention . . . this is to be Our Last Supper. Now watch and learn how a proper cook works!

Tippi *snaps the lighter closed and puts everything back into her purse. No cigarette.*

She waits. Poised and cool.

Meanwhile, **Reeves** *lights the joint. He uses an expensive saucer from the kitchen as an ashtray.*

Vincent   No ashtray?

A voice surprises **Tippi***:*

Hitch   No ashtray.

Alfred Hitchcock *enters from the other part of the house. He's been watching her.*

He wears a dark suit, white shirt, dark tie.

Hitch *is pink and rotund, speaks and moves deliberately. He has carefully manufactured a persona of sublime, sardonic disinterest . . . He has a mischievous schoolboy's sense of humor and enjoys shocking with off-color and provocative remarks. He is also, it goes without saying, a cinematic genius.*

His eyes almost never leave her.

You saw there was no ashtray. Your eyes went to the table. Then to the bar. Surely there was an ashtray there last night? Then back to the flame. What will The Girl do? Will she rebel? Displease? Hide the ashes in a drawer guiltily; hoping Mrs. Danvers won't discover them? Or bugger the floor and flick the ashes there? What a bitch.

Tippi   Please. It's been a long day.

Reeves (*finds a saucer*)   Don't seem to have an ashtray. This'll do.

Hitch   The green scarf was intended for the green suit. You see, they match.

Tippi   I like it with this.

Vincent (*re: the saucer/ashtray*)   You can't actually tell me you're using Spode for your spliff?!

Reeves   I like it.

Vincent *and* **Hitch** (*simultaneously*)   At your peril.

Vincent *and* **Reeves** *continue cooking as* **Tippi** *removes the scarf and tucks it into her purse.*

Hitch *is pleased . . . He goes to the bar area.*

Hitch   Miss Head spent too much time on your personal wardrobe for us to make elemental mistakes as to color.

Tippi   It's not a costume. It's real life.

Hitch   Nonetheless, the palette holds.

He pours champagne.

Tippi   I shouldn't. I have an engagement tonight and—it's been such a long day.

Hitch   But we have to rehearse, my dear. And there's dinner . . . (*Hands her champagne.*) . . . Engagement?

Tippi   Just a drink with a friend.

Hitch   Just a drink with a friend in a grey suit with matching three-quarter gloves and pearl—that strand's too long for evening by the way—and Givenchy shoes, small scuff on the left toe. Would you like to telephone your regrets?

Tippi   No, no. It's all right.

Hitch   Have to keep focused these last weeks. Keep things . . . in hand.

She's uncomfortable . . . Subtly moves around the room trying to find a place to fit in.

Hitch   Did you enjoy today?

Tippi   Yeah, was good, fine. Rear projection's always a little funny . . . Seems so unreal.

Hitch   Unlike the rest of moviemaking?

Tippi   I mean pretend roads and pretend cars. I don't know what I mean. I'm awfully tired; these hours are . . . Maybe I should just go home. It would be better if I went home.

Hitch   Heavens, I only make these silly movies so we can dine at the end of the day, didn't you know that?

He smiles.

Tonight the cook has prepared a veritable orgy for the senses . . . (*He relishes the sound and the anticipation of the menu.*) . . . We are to begin with consommé and petites quenelles, followed by poached eggs in Chartreuse sauce, oysters Rockefeller, lamb rolls and pâté with maître d'hôtel butter and peas à l'étouffée, and for dessert a slice of le marquis au chocolat topped with crème au beurre l'Anglaise . . . Peasant food really.

Tippi   I can't eat so much when I'm working, you know that.

Hitch   Do you intend me to eat it all?

Tippi   You should if you want.

Hitch   Don't you think I'm fat enough?

Tippi   No—I—

Hitch   A quick bite. We'll have a quick bite, won't we?

Tippi   Yes, yes.

Hitch   Quick bite.

Tippi   Yes.

Hitch   Do you think I'm fat?

Tippi   No.

Hitch   What would you call it then?

Tippi   I don't know.

Hitch   Would you prefer "big-boned"? . . . or "healthy"?

Tippi   Yes.

Hitch   "Robust"?

Tippi   Sure.

Hitch   "Husky"?

Tippi   Sure.

Hitch   Anything but "pudgy."

Tippi   Yes.

Hitch   Do you think I'm "healthy"?

Tippi   I don't know.

Hitch   Shall we settle for "jolly"?

Tippi   Okay.

She nervously pulls out her cigarettes again, puts them away.

Beat.

He removes a cigarette lighter from his pocket . . . Holds it up.

Lights it. The flame burns.

He stands there.

She pulls out a cigarette and crosses the room to him.

She leans in, lights the cigarette.

Hitch   Is that lipstick from the picture?

Tippi   No. It's mine.

Hitch   Grace Kelly used to put a little line of pale color right here on the middle of her lower lip. She said a lady should always look like she's just swallowed cum and there's a drop left on her mouth.

Tippi *tries not to react.*

Hitch   Princess Grace that is.

He smiles and removes an ashtray from a drawer. Sets it on a table in the living room and sits on the sofa.

Hitch   I have some exciting news.

Tippi   Yes?

Hitch   Can you feign more enthusiasm?

Tippi   Sorry. What?

Hitch   This news will delight you. Titillate you.

Tippi   I'm poised.

He enjoys her droll use of the word.

Hitch   Very well then. One likes to have the audience leaning forward . . . I have commissioned Jay Allen to write a screen adaptation of *Mary Rose*, the J. M. Barrie play. It is the role of a lifetime and I've been waiting for an actress who could essay it. For *Mary Rose* I have awaited a *muse*, that person who will spark my imagination to places as yet unforeseen . . . Not Madeleine Carroll, nor Ingrid Bergman, nor Joan Fontaine, nor the sperm-spattered Grace Kelly . . . *You* will be my Mary Rose. Have I told you the story?

Tippi   Yes.

Hitch   We're in Scottish waters, Outer Hebrides, well past the 58th parallel, as remote as a place can be . . . we push through the mists; an island appears, this is a matte painting and process shot . . . Morning light catches the crags and promontories. There's no music, just the lonely whistle of the wind, the *forlorn* whistle of the wind . . . (*He makes the lonely sound.*) . . . Immediately we know we're in a haunted place, a place of sad reckoning, wherein a climax shall occur

perhaps this very night! . . . We move closer to the island . . .
Voice-over of The Girl . . . "When I lost myself on the island,
time stopped for me, but not for the world . . . I was ageless,
but life aged around me . . . Was I blessed or cursed? Can
you tell me?"

She looks at him.

Hitch   It's symbolic.

Tippi   Mmm.

Hitch   It's about love.

Tippi   Mmm.

Hitch   Eternal love.

Tippi   Ah.

Hitch   Do you believe that?

Tippi   What?

Hitch   Is love eternal?

Tippi   Is that rhetorical?

Hitch   Not necessarily.

Tippi   Love is eternal.

Hitch   True love. Not the sham we settle for most of the
time . . . that rear projection passion . . . In a way, *Mary Rose*
is about the agelessness of movies too . . . Take you, for
example.

Beat.

She is very tense. He does not seem to notice.

Tippi   How so?

Hitch   What have I done for you?

Tippi   I don't understand.

Hitch   Since we first met. What have I done for you?

Tippi   . . . You know what you've done.

Hitch   I want to hear you say it.

Tippi   You've done everything.

Hitch   Shot by shot. Tell me the story.

He folds his hands over his belly and looks at her.

Tippi   . . . I came from New York—

Hitch   "She" came. The character came.

Tippi   She came from New York. She's a model, not an actress. She's not a kid anymore. She's got a kid to feed in fact, a daughter. She doesn't know much of anyone. She does some modeling . . . You see her in a TV commercial and you ask to meet her, and then you sign her. You pick out her clothes and remake her look and teach her how to act on camera . . . You gave her confidence. You gave her *The Birds* and *Marnie* . . . You believed in her.

He's a mesmerizing storyteller:

Hitch   *I made her immortal* . . . She will always be Melanie Daniels or Marnie or Mary Rose, frozen in time as the world ages around her . . . always *poised* at the ripe edge of perfection on the screen . . . Heartbreaking in a way, for she herself will grow old. Wrinkles will appear. Her daughter will grow up and get married. Her friends will die. I will die. She will get old, like me. Maybe she'll understand me a little more then and be a shade kinder in her memory, more generous than I deserve . . . But then the final reel . . . One sunny day she's walking past a revival house. We follow her shoes walking along the pavement. Click-click-click. The shoes stop. Why, we wonder. Hold for a beat. We move up the back of her legs, the seams of her stockings, up her back, to the nape of her neck, and then the back of her head. She's looking up. Cut to her POV . . . a marquee. Her name! It's one of her old pictures! . . . Cut back to her face . . . big close-up . . . She's thinking. Does she dare go in? . . .

Suspense . . . Yessss . . . Then she goes into the darkened cinema and sits, anonymous among the other spectators. The picture begins . . . The flickering light overhead . . . Ahhh . . . And there she is again. As she was. Endlessly young and beautiful. Luminous. Flawless . . . Remember her?

Tippi *is touched.*

Beat.

Hitch   You must not wear that scarf with anything but the ensemble for which it was designed.

Tippi (*smiles*)   All right.

Hitch   Why don't you take off your shoes, that scuff is distressing me.

She slips off her shoes.

Hitch   Would you be good enough to fetch me another glass of champagne?

Tippi   I shouldn't stay, really . . .

Hitch   But we must rehearse, my dear. This is your job.

She goes and gets him another glass of champagne.

Tippi   I'd think you'd like to spend an evening with your wife and daughter.

Hitch   They understand my work.

Tippi   Yes. That's why we're here. *We're working*.

Hitch   You sound like you're convincing yourself.

Tippi   Or you.

*Then, from in the kitchen area, as **Vincent** and **Reeves** cook:*

Reeves   Do you miss your wife and daughter?

Vincent   What?

Reeves   Do you miss your wife and daughter when you're away filming?

Vincent   They understand my work.

Reeves   That's not what I asked you.

Tippi   Still, don't you miss all the evenings with them?

Hitch   They understand my work.

Tippi   That's not what I asked you.

Reeves   I asked if you missed them.

Hitch *and* **Vincent** (*simultaneously*)   Don't be silly.

Hitch (*changing the subject*)   Now where did I put those sketches?

Vincent *changes the subject by dramatically pronouncing judgment on the fish*:

Vincent   It's a catastrophe!

Tippi *returns with the champagne, sits with* **Hitch**, *folds her legs under her on the sofa. He is content.*

Reeves   Can a fish really be a catastrophe?

Vincent   Ask Captain Ahab.

Hitch   Here, I've some storyboards for *Mary Rose* . . .

He shows her some sketches as **Reeves** *and* **Vincent** *sample the fish.*

Reeves   Well, it's, um—

Vincent   Apocalyptic.

Tippi (*re: storyboards*)   These are gorgeous.

Reeves (*re: fish*)   It's good.

Hitch   You have taste.

Vincent   You have no taste.

Tippi *and* **Reeves** (*simultaneously*)   Thank you.

Hitch   You have to let them wash over you.

Vincent   Let the flavors settle and you'll see.

Reeves   Come on, it's not that awful.

Tippi   Wash over me . . .?

Vincent   Here's how you cook fish . . . you carry it through a warm room and serve.

He dumps the fish into the trash without another word and then busies himself in the kitchen area.

Hitch *and* **Tippi** *continues looking at the storyboards quietly as . . .*

Throughout the following **Vincent** *finds an apron, sorts through the fridge and cabinets, and prepares an impromptu dish: simple but elegant pasta with a lemon cream sauce . . . He is a master chef.*

Vincent   Now listen, Michael, you're a talented kid. Maybe you'll have a great future in the movies, but it's not working out with us. Chalk it up to "creative differences." There's no point in beating a dead horse—although I'm sure you'd like to add it to the catalog of depravities in the picture.

Reeves   Is that what you think *Witchfinder General* is? A catalog of depravities?

Vincent   Well, let's see . . . You open on a hanging. Then you go to a shooting. Then you torture the old priest. Then the first rape. Then the second rape. Then back to torturing the old priest. Then the rats. Then the drowning. Then the other hanging. Then the burning. Then the other shooting. And then the ending, which would make Titus Andronicus puke . . . Could you find some butter and heat that skillet?

Tippi (*re: the storyboards*)   Gosh, that's majestic.

Hitch   'Gosh'? You're so bloody American.

Reeves *prepares the butter as . . .*

Reeves   So the film's bloody. Violence is bloody.

Vincent   But there's got to be a limit or it's nothing but pornography.

Reeves (*jumps on this*)   That's what it is! Violence is pornographic. Why do we continue to treat brutality as if it's a joke? It's not. It's not the old Kensington Gore, it's not John Wayne shooting Indians with antiseptic cleanliness— violence is sickening and that's what our film is going to show.

Vincent   It's make-believe, Michael.

Reeves   It's immoral. You punch someone in the face and it breaks their teeth. You smash a chair over someone's head they're going to bleed and likely have brain damage and spinal injuries for the rest of their lives. It's about time we showed that in the cinema.

Vincent   Why would anyone pay to see that?

Reeves   Because it's real.

Vincent   Oh listen to her.

Reeves   We don't live in Oz anymore. Dorothy's all grown up. Fred Astaire's not tap dancing on the ceiling and Bela Lugosi isn't scary. You know what's scary? Vietnam.

Vincent   Here we go . . .

Reeves   Serious cinema's about discomfort now . . . About provocation and contemporary relevance.

Vincent   I don't go to the pictures to be upset, I go to be entertained.

Reeves   That's not true. You don't admit it, because you've been disappointed so many times in the past—we all have, our hearts have been broken by too many frivolous movies— but you go the cinema for the same reason you look at paintings—(*He points to the Turner.*)—you want to be touched, *you want to feel*.

Vincent   Yes, but I don't want to feel *bad*!

Reeves   Of course you do. Why are we still watching *Hamlet* four hundred years later? We want to cry . . . we want to feel something *deeply*. We can't resist the gravitational pull of tragedy.

Vincent   All young men love tragedy . . . When you get older you'll learn that you can't feel everything so deeply all the time. And sometimes it's better not to feel anything at all.

This strikes **Reeves** *. . .* **Vincent** *covers the moment; continues to concoct the impromptu meal . . . He tosses* **Reeves** *some lemons then places a skillet over the boiling pasta water to melt the butter.*

Vincent   Always melt butter for a cream sauce like so . . . the steam melts the butter more gently and it doesn't separate, which is abhorrent.

Reeves (*re: the lemons*)   What do you want me to do with these?

Vincent   Finely grate two peels.

Hitch (*re: the storyboards*)   That's a matte painting. Or location on Catalina. But I abhor boats.

Tippi   You could take a plane.

Hitch   I abhor flight.

Tippi   You're big on abhorrence.

Hitch   Too hard to rehearse on location anyway.

Reeves *grates the lemon peels as . . .*

Reeves   I want to rehearse.

Vincent   What?

Reeves   I want to rehearse the scene for tomorrow.

Vincent   Suddenly he's Stanislavski.

Reeves   Listen—

Vincent   And there is no "tomorrow"—*I'm leaving, Michael.*

Reeves   I know I'm not terribly good with actors; it's awkward for me, but I want to make myself a better director.

Vincent   You're transparent.

Reeves   Give me a chance to learn from you.

Vincent   Now desperate.

Reeves   Please.

Vincent   Day late and a dollar short, pal. My car comes at eight tomorrow to take me to the station and thence to London and thence to the good old US of A to my aforementioned wife and daughter. You should have fucking "respected my process" three weeks ago instead of insulting me at every turn.

Reeves   I didn't mean to—

Vincent   Of course you did! You didn't want me for the part, the studio insisted, you wanted to make your movie so you were stuck with me—which you've been telling everyone on the set every chance you get, which is pretty degrading I will add, so why don't you get goddamn Donald Pleasence and rehearse with him!

Reeves   So it's your pride?

Vincent   Not just that. I've been making pictures for longer than you've been alive and have some *standing* in the industry, a *reputation* among my peers!

Reeves   Which is what? Your reputation?

Vincent   *Professional*.

Reeves   What jobs did you do in the past two years?

Vincent   What?

Reeves   You heard me.

Vincent   I don't see the point.

Reeves   Go on. What jobs did you do? . . . You're a professional. You remember.

Vincent *looks at him. Knows exactly what* **Reeves** *is up to.*

Then, with a good stab at dignity:

Vincent   *Tomb of Ligeia . . . War-Gods of the Deep . . . The Jackals . . . House of a Thousand Dolls . . . Dr. Goldfoot and the Bikini Machine . . . Dr. Goldfoot and the Girl Bombs . . .* and the first few weeks of a misbegotten little shocker called *Witchfinder General.*

Reeves   My God you have been busy . . . All in two years.

Vincent *cooks; doesn't respond.*

They work on the dish for a moment.

Reeves   And on television? In the last two years.

Beat.

Vincent   *The Man from U.N.C.L.E . . . The Red Skelton Hour . . . The Danny Kaye Show . . . Voyage to the Bottom of the Sea . . . F Troop.*

Reeves   Egg-xactly.

Vincent   And *Batman.*

Reeves   Does it bother you that everyone my age only knows you as Egghead?

Vincent   You missed my Timon of Athens?

Reeves   Go on, joke.

Vincent   Congratulations, you've caught me out: *I enjoy working!* God help me the day I don't. Here's my fondest wish . . . to drop dead in the middle of a scene and be carried from the stage and plopped in the ground still in my pancake—*still in the game.*

Reeves   So it's quantity you're after, not quality?

Vincent   Longevity.

Reeves   What about taste?

Vincent   Let me tell you, kid, I'm a *working actor*. I've supported myself and my family from the time I was twenty . . . I didn't have your advantages, Mr. Reeves. Some of us weren't born quite so rich. Some of us actually had to work for a living.

Reeves   Some of us used to actually act for a living too.

Vincent   Oh how droll.

Reeves   All those Edgar Allan Poe films for Roger Corman. All that smirking over-the-top melodrama, the cape flourishing and eyebrow raising. No one takes it seriously, least of all you, and worst of everything: *the audience knows*. They know you're only fooling . . . "It's just me, old Vinnie Price; we both know this is a bit of a lark. No one's really going to get hurt. *Nothing to be scared of, loves*." You've become a winking caricature of yourself.

Vincent   This is a hell of a way to get me to stay on your picture.

Reeves   Go on, tell me I'm wrong. Tell me you're not debasing yourself by doing so much junk. At least with this film I'm trying to get you to act again, *like it matters*.

Vincent *refills their glasses, hands a glass of wine to* **Reeves**.

A beat as **Vincent** *considers him.*

Vincent   What frightens you?

Reeves   What?

Vincent   Indulge me. What frightens you?

Reeves   Indifference.

Vincent   What else?

Reeves   Insignificance.

Vincent   That's better . . . Go on.

Reeves   Not you. You don't frighten me. That's the bloody problem. You don't frighten anyone!

Vincent   Go on . . . Indifference . . . Insignificance . . .

Reeves   *Artistic compromise.*

Vincent   Oh good for you! Won't Godard be proud?

Reeves   This is pointless.

Vincent   Not to me.

Reeves   My fears don't matter. Only what the audience fears.

Vincent (*relentlessly*)   There's no audience here. What frightens you?

Reeves   You mean spiders and the like?

Vincent   I mean the truth.

Reeves   *Madness.*

It's like a sudden bolt of truth.

Reeves   Despair . . . Loneliness. Dogs. Horses. England. America. Snakes. Producers. Nembutal. Lithium. Phenobarbital. Librium. Valium. Electroshock. This house. Outside this house. Being on the set. Not being on the set. No vision. No point of view. No point . . . Failure . . . Expectation . . . Age.

Vincent   Ah.

Reeves   That's the one you were waiting for?

Vincent   I knew it would come . . . Every twenty-four-year-old in the world fears twenty-five more than anything. It's written all over your face.

Reeves   What is?

Vincent   *"What if?"* . . . What if he walks and my movie falls apart? What if my career ends before it's begun? What if no one will hire me again? What if twenty-five is worse than twenty-four—and twenty-six worse still? It could happen. Happens all the time . . . So what if all your hopes and dreams *don't* come true? What will your life be then? . . . You see, at my age my hopes and dreams have already happened. I have arrived at myself. You're still hoping you will . . . But what if you don't, Michael?

Reeves *looks at him, a bit shaken.*

Beat.

Vincent   Are you sure I don't frighten you?

Beat.

Then, from the living room . . .

Tippi   I'm sorry . . . my lipstick. Ever since you mentioned my lipstick . . .

She pulls out a compact and checks her makeup.

Hitch   It's a compulsion.

Reeves (*peering closer at* **Vincent**)   Are you wearing makeup?

Tippi *and* **Vincent** (*simultaneously*)   What?

Hitch   Checking your face. It's a compulsion.

Reeves   Are you wearing makeup?

Vincent   Is it melting?

He checks his makeup in a pot lid as **Tippi** *checks hers in the compact.*

Tippi   It's not a compulsion, it's part of my job.

Vincent   Gods. I look like a corpse in need of a mortician.

Reeves   Why do you wear it?

Tippi   I have to look young.

Hitch   Young*er*.

Vincent   Hide the lines, old boy.

Tippi   No one wants to look old.

Reeves   Are you afraid of getting old?

Hitch   You're vain.

Vincent   Ask me that when you're my age.

Tippi *and* **Vincent** (*simultaneously*)   Everyone's vain.

Reeves   It's a mask, to protect yourself.

Tippi   Don't make too much of it.

Hitch   Vanity is a minor vice, like kicking the cat.

Vincent   Who wants to face the world without a little mascara?

Tippi   You wouldn't like me without makeup.

Hitch   I've never seen you without it.

Reeves   Wonder what you look without it, just as you.

Vincent   You'll never know.

Tippi   I'm rarely without it.

Reeves   I'd like to see that.

Hitch   When might you be without it?

Reeves   There's an honesty about a raw face, isn't there?

Tippi   First thing in the morning, I guess.

Reeves   When you look at the glass when you wake up.

Hitch   There's a provocative thought.

Vincent   I avoid the mirror at all costs.

Reeves   I don't.

Tippi   Do you like looking in the mirror?

Vincent   You're very young.

Hitch   I'm too old.

Tippi   Old faces are honest.

Reeves   Old faces can be beautiful.

Hitch   Spoken like a young person.

Vincent   Now you're just flirting.

Reeves   Is it working?

Vincent   I'll let you know . . . Now, let's have us some chow!

With a hearty flourish, **Vincent** *removes the apron and prepares two plates. They move away to eat the pasta dish they have prepared as . . .*

Hitch *pulls himself up from the sofa, never an easy task, and he and* **Tippi** *move to the kitchen area . . .*

Hitch   Ugh. I find that a prodigious amount of physical labor without proper sustenance can lead only to ruin.

Tippi   Was that physical labor?

Hitch   Believe me.

Vincent   And before you sink into an abyss of jejune Freudianism, I wear makeup to look less corpse-like, which is my natural pallor.

Reeves   You're in the right business then.

Vincent   Horror films, you mean.

Reeves   Acting. All the time apparently.

Vincent   Oh, isn't he piquant?

They eat, as in the kitchen area:

Tippi   *Mary Rose* is going to be a wonderful movie. Thank you for showing me the pictures.

Hitch   I planned to do it first with Madeleine Carroll, did I mention that? Then she became pregnant, always *catastrophic* for an actress, distends the cervix . . . Mind you, this was forty years ago. Longer than you've been alive I've wanted to tell this story . . . Sooner or later, I get what I want.

The point is not lost on her.

Hitch *pulls various elaborate dishes from the fridge, stove, oven, and warming trays. He arranges the beautiful serving pieces on a counter with a keen directorial eye as . . .*

Hitch   But I had to find the right actress. My *muse* if you will. Art and Eros, always superimposed, don't you find? You cannot separate the two: the model naked in supplication before the artist; the artist exposing himself in trust. The beast of creation is always erect.

Tippi   Is it?

Hitch   Would we have "Ode to a Nightingale" if Keats had not desired Fanny Brawne? Would Diaghilev have commissioned *Rite of Spring* without his lust for Nijinsky? And could Nijinsky have danced so powerfully without Diaghilev's nakedness before him? Touching the muse and touching the flesh must be one in the same.

Tippi   Maybe he just saw a bird.

Hitch   What?

Tippi   Maybe Keats just saw a nightingale and wrote a poem?

Hitch   You know better.

Tippi   The bird is a metaphor, I understand that. But why does it all have to come down to wanting sex? There are other things.

Hitch   Nothing that hurts so much . . . Facing desire, looking into the eyes of "*La belle dame sans merci*" . . . The real question perhaps is this . . . we know how the bird inspired Keats, but how did Keats inspire the bird, Miss Hedren?

She is increasingly anxious about all of this.

Hitch *arranges the last few serving pieces on the counters.*

Hitch   In any event, *Mary Rose* . . . After Madeleine Carroll's inopportune maternity it was to be with Joan Fontaine . . . then Ingrid . . . then Grace . . . And now you . . . You shall be my Mary Rose, the apotheosis of them all, sparking my imagination to places as yet unforeseen.

Tippi *doesn't respond.*

Hitch (*alert*)   Did you hear me?

Tippi   Yes, yes, of course.

Hitch   You shall be my Mary Rose.

Tippi   Well, we'll see.

Hitch *carefully shifts the dishes around on the counter, creating new patterns, troubled by her evasive response.*

Hitch   Tonight the cook has prepared for our delectation a meal that begins with consommé and petites quenelles, followed as I mentioned by—*What do you mean "we'll see"?*

Tippi *looks over the many dishes.*

Tippi   I can't decide.

She is suddenly in tears.

Tippi   There are too many. And all so—beyond me, beyond what I know—I can't decide. I'm so tired. This food is too rich, I told you I can't eat that much. I can't eat anything. I'm so tense at work I throw everything up. They had to take in the white dress, did you know that? I can't do this anymore. *You can't do this to me.*

Hitch *hands her his handkerchief and then, seemingly, ignores the breakdown:*

Hitch   Kiss kiss kill kill, eh?

As he speaks, he puts on the apron, sorts through the cupboards and fridge. He begins making two simple but elegant light sandwiches . . . **Hitch**, *like* **Vincent**, *is a master chef.*

Hitch   Don't all my films come down to that? Admittedly, the order varies . . . Kiss kiss kill kill . . . Kill kill kiss kiss . . . Kiss kill kiss kill . . . You can end on the kiss or you can end on the kill. That's the big decision. *Psycho* and *Vertigo*, by way of example, end on the kill, on the madness. *North by Northwest* and *Rear Window* end on the kiss, on the resumption of a sane universe.

She has no idea where he is going, dries her eyes. He continues to prepare the sandwiches.

Hitch   Where would you say *Marnie* ends?

Tippi   Well . . . she's traumatized, but the suggestion is she's on the road to recovery with Mark . . . I think it's meant to be a kiss.

Hitch   I agree. Do you like the odd cold cut?

Tippi   What do you mean?

Hitch   Luncheon meat.

Tippi   Yes.

Hitch   Ham, specifically.

Tippi   Yes.

Hitch   Love ham, aside from Robert Newton . . . (*He continues with the sandwiches.*) . . . I think Marnie has to *earn* her kiss. It doesn't come easily. Because she is so psychologically damaged she must go through a crucible to be cured, she must be tested. She has to suffer. We all have to suffer if we're to earn our kiss, don't we, Miss Hedren? Thus the scene in the stateroom we're rehearsing tonight—it's the electroshock she needs to emerge sane at the end.

Tippi   Does she?

Hitch   What?

Tippi   Emerge sane?

He's intrigued by the question.

Tippi   She's a compulsive thief, sexually repressed; hiding her identity and her emotions from the first shot . . . her hair's dyed; her clothes are costumes; her name's fake. There's nothing real about her. It's all makeup. She's *hollow* . . . Then she meets a man who becomes fascinated with her. She rejects him. He doesn't stop. It gets romantic as they work together but she keeps rejecting him, won't sleep with him; won't touch him. He more or less blackmails her into marrying him. They go on a sea cruise for their honeymoon, so he can get her completely isolated, away from family and friends, so she's even more vulnerable. She rejects him again. He rapes her. She tries to kill herself. He finally takes her back to the root of her psychological trauma. She relives it. They drive off together . . . That's what the film's about.

Hitch   That's what the film *shows*, that's not what it *is*.

Tippi   I just think he's broken her down so he can possess her more fully. So he can remake her the way he wants . . . so he can *Vertigo* her.

Hitch   But . . . she's cured . . . It's meant to be a happy ending you know!

Tippi   Hitch . . . He controls her. He manipulates her. He follows her. He spies on her. He blackmails her. He makes her financially dependent on him. He cuts off all her other relationships. *He rapes her* . . . One trauma replaced by another.

Hitch   He protects her.

Tippi   Is that what he's trying to do?

Hitch   He doesn't want her to suffer. He doesn't want her to go on being hollow. He wants to bring his rich life experience to her, to share that with her, he has so much to offer.

Tippi   He wants to possess her. Why in God's name doesn't he just let her go when she begs him to?!

Hitch   Because he loves her.

Tippi   He's *obsessed* with her. That's not the same.

Hitch   He wants to fuck her.

Tippi   He could fuck anyone.

Hitch   But it's her. She's the one. She's The Girl.

Tippi   Her damage excites him.

Hitch   Yes!

Tippi   But then what if she really is cured at the end? What happens when the damage goes away? What will excite him then? . . . She's just like any other girl now, not the luxuriously complicated neurotic she was. What's going to fascinate him? Isn't he going to lose interest? . . . Isn't he going to realize how impossible this all has been? *How sad?*

Hitch   That's after the credits, so doesn't matter. Now let's have some chow.

He slices and then presents the two simple but elegant sandwiches he has prepared.

She is grateful. It's a sweet gesture.

They stand and eat the sandwiches.

Hitch   Wouldn't that be easier without the gloves?

Tippi   Oh, yes.

They continue eating. Oddly, she does not remove the gloves.

Tippi   After the credits roll . . . Sometimes that's the best movie of all . . . the one in your head.

Hitch   You forget; they're all in my head.

Tippi   So what happens to Marnie after the movie ends?

Hitch   After the movie she ceases to exist.

Tippi   "*What if?*" . . . Don't you ever play "what if?" What if *Marnie* continued? What would happen to her?

Hitch   To *them*. They are together. Marnie and Mark. Alliteratively linked if nothing else. *Inexorably* linked.

Tippi   I doubt that.

Hitch   Oh?

Tippi   Mmm.

Hitch   Don't be so enigmatic.

Tippi   I thought you liked mysteries.

Hitch   All right then, you tell me, Miss Hedren. What happens to Marnie after the picture ends? *What if?*

Beat . . . This is serious now.

Tippi   She walks away . . . He's given her confidence. He's made her strong enough to leave him. So she does.

Hitch   She can't.

Tippi   She will.

Hitch   Why?

Tippi   She doesn't love him.

Hitch   She could try.

Tippi   She can't force her heart.

Hitch   She could open herself to him. Allow the possibility of a future together . . . "'What if?"

Tippi   There is no more "what if?" . . . That ended when he assaulted her . . . Be honest, he only wanted her to make him feel young again. He never cared about what she wanted . . . She was just The Girl.

She looks at him.

She slowly removes her gloves.

Her hands are covered with an ugly red rash.

Tippi   They cover it with makeup, so you won't see. They don't want to upset you. No one wants to upset you. You're so protected in that chair of yours . . . It's dermatitis of some sort. It actually increases in size with tension and anxiety. Three weeks ago it was just a little spot. Now it's growing . . . where will it end? . . . Isn't that suspenseful?

She holds her hands up to him.

See what you've done to me?

Then, from where they have just finished eating:

Reeves   Do you know what it'll do to me?

Vincent   What?

Reeves   Leaving the picture! It'll ruin me!

Vincent   Now you're frightened.

Tippi (*re: her rash*)   Does this frighten you?

Hitch   Is it contagious?

Tippi   Oh yes.

Hitch   Please put your gloves on.

Tippi   Yes, Mr. Hitchcock.

She puts her gloves back on . . . Then she and **Hitch**, *grimly silent, clear away the dishes as he plans his next moves.*

Meanwhile, **Vincent** *and* **Reeves** *continue*:

Reeves   Then let me ask you a question. What about you? What frightens *you*?

Vincent   Slim-hipped directors in turtlenecks.

Reeves (*smiles*)   No, I mean it.

Vincent   I'll tell you what frightened me when I was a kid . . . Lon Chaney in *Phantom of the Opera*, the unmasking scene . . .

He acts it out briefly, then . . .

Vincent   Beyond camp now, with that Chautauqua-orator's hand, like Hitler gone fruit, but back in the day that was terror!

Reeves   I meant what scares you outside of movies.

Vincent   There's something outside of movies?

Reeves   Anyhow, that's not terror. Here's terror . . . *Freaks*. Tod Browning, 1932.

Vincent   *Dead of Night*.

Reeves   *Peeping Tom*.

Vincent   *The Innocents*.

Reeves   *Cul-de-sac*.

Vincent   *The Haunting*.

Reeves   *Mad Love*.

Vincent   *Island of Lost Souls*.

Reeves and **Vincent** (*simultaneously*)   *Psycho*!

Vincent   "A boy's best friend is his mother . . ."

Reeves   "We all go a little mad sometimes."

Vincent   Who knew you were such an old horror queen?

Reeves   Not for long. I'm going to get out of the genre as soon as I can.

Vincent   If I had a nickel . . .

Reeves *smiles, goes to the living room area as . . .*

Reeves   And of course my favorite movie quote ever . . .
"You want to know something? I don't think Mozart's going
to help at all."

Vincent   . . . Hmm . . . Is it horror?

Reeves   Not precisely.

Vincent   You've stumped me. What is it?

Reeves *picks up a script, holds it out.*

Reeves   You'll have to earn the answer . . . Come rehearse.

Vincent   Forget it.

Reeves   It'll drive you crazy trying to remember.

Vincent   Drop dead, buster!

Reeves   You know it will.

Vincent *looks at him.*

Reeves *shakes the script at him.*

Vincent   You're serious?

Reeves   I'm treating you like a proper actor, like you want.

Vincent   As opposed to like cattle, like you want . . . This
isn't going to make a difference. I'm still leaving tomorrow.

Reeves   As you like.

Vincent   Let me get fortified.

He pours himself a huge glass of red wine as **Reeves** *takes a pill.*

Vincent   What's that?

Reeves   Largactil. Anti-depressant.

Vincent   Is that why your hands shake sometimes?

Reeves   My hands don't shake.

Vincent   Of course they do.

He joins **Reeves***; puts on his glasses and takes the script.*

Vincent   You're going to read her I take it, heaving bosom and all?

Reeves   I'll do my best. We'll start with the bit at the end, those lines before they go; from 'Sara Lowes, you have been accused' . . . (*Awkwardly preparing.*) . . . All right, relax now; shake your arms out or something . . . Okay . . . Ready? . . . Hmm . . . Deep breath. Settle. Let's just give it a nice, easy read, eeeeeeasy.

Vincent   You're a dab hand at this rehearsal business.

He clears his throat and begins.

"Sara Lowes, you have been accused this day of consorting with your master, the Devil. Confess your sins or you will suffer the pains of the damned."

Reeves   "I am no witch, Matthew Hopkins."

Vincent   "Master Stearne will soon prove it otherwise, as legal writ and precedent dictate. Take her to the rack! And may God have mercy on your soul."

Reeves   Well . . . Well, well, well, well, well, well, well . . . *Well!* . . . Let's start at the top, shall we?

Vincent   "Sara Lowes—"

Reeves   There's no balcony.

Vincent   What?

Reeves   Sorry. Never mind. Go ahead.

Vincent   "Sara Lowes, you have been—"

Reeves   Stop projecting.

Vincent   What?!

Reeves   You're not in the Putney Hippodrome.

Vincent   The what?!

Reeves   Never mind, never mind . . . sorry . . . Whenever you're ready.

Vincent   "Sara Lowes, you have been accused—"

Reeves   I mean less projection, less elocution . . . Microphone's right here.

Vincent   Is it really?!

Reeves   I mean less voice.

Vincent   Less voice?

Reeves   Less *that* voice.

Vincent   Less *that* voice?

Reeves   The buttery one.

Vincent   Less butter?

Reeves   No butter.

Vincent   Less voice, no butter, let me tell you, you're . . . fucking Billy Wilder, kid . . . "Sara Lowes, you have been accused this day of consorting with your master, the Devil—"

Reeves   Vincent, take it down a bit. Don't say dev-IL. Just devil. Just say devil. Like that. Devil. Like a real person. Like a fucking real person not one of those goddamn Poe characters!

Vincent   Don't push it, Alice.

Reeves   Sorry, sorry, go on . . . Whenever you're ready.

Vincent   "Sara Lowes, you have been accused this day of consorting with your master, the Devil. Confess your sins or you will suffer the pains of the damned."

Beat.

Vincent *looks at him.*

IT'S YOUR LINE!

Reeves   Christ—"I am no witch, Matthew Hopkins."

Vincent   Oh well done, Thespis is weeping . . . "Master Stearne will soon prove it otherwise, as legal writ and precedent dictate. Take her to the rack! And may God have mercy on your soul."

Reeves   There—it's that smile. That little pause and smirk before you say, "Take her to the rack!" That's what I don't want.

Vincent   The line is, "Take her to the rack!" What the fuck am I supposed to do with it?!

Reeves   You're right. The line's too florid. Make it just, "Take her!" A direct order . . . calculating, commanding. "Take her!"

Vincent   "Master Stearne will soon prove it otherwise, as legal writ and precedent dictate. Take her! And may God have mercy on your soul."

Reeves   Still too much emphasis. I want you do to less.

Vincent   You want me to do less?

Reeves   Yes.

Vincent   How much less?

Reeves   Nothing.

Vincent   You want me to do nothing?

Reeves   Nothing.

Vincent   How much nothing?

Reeves   Very little nothing.

Vincent   Ah.

Reeves   No eye-rolling. No lip-smacking. No cape-twirling. No eyebrow-raising. No Roger Corman. No Roderick Usher . . . I want you to be a cipher, Vincent . . . Matthew Hopkins is a figure of inexorable vindictiveness.

Vincent   Why?

Reeves   Why what?

Vincent   Why is he a figure of "inexorable vindictiveness"?

Reeves   I don't know. It's inexplicable.

Vincent   Inexplicable inexorable vindictiveness. I don't know if that's actable.

Reeves   Look . . . I can't talk about the character's motivation or anything, that's your job. Why he does what he does, I haven't a clue; I would only be making it up on the spot to try and please you . . .

He is serious now, trying to explain.

I can't tell you *why* he is, but I can tell you *what* he is, this Witchfinder General . . . He's one of those petty functionaries in Spandau, given license for his sadism by the state. But I just don't see him like an actor does—I can't.

Vincent   How do you see him then?

Reeves   Well . . . like a director I suppose.

Vincent   Which is what?

Reeves   For me it's not cerebral or biographical or dramaturgical, it's ocular. I *see* him in images. Or more like jump cuts . . . like the shower scene in *Psycho*: low angle, high angle, insert, wide shot, mid-shot, close-up.

Vincent   What are the images?

Reeves   They're random.

Vincent   It'll help me.

Reeves   Really, I don't—

Vincent   Go on, anything you see.

Reeves *closes his eyes; this becomes unexpectedly emotional and personal for him*:

Reeves   . . . Brown earth, dried . . . Nothing growing . . .
Winter . . . Long shot. Figure alone on a moor, silhouetted
against the grey sky. No, not a moor, a battlefield, and you
can see all the way to the horizon. It's not the Battle of
Naseby like in the film. No. Too many bodies for that, he
could walk over them for a mile and never set foot on the
ground . . . Getting closer. Zooming in. Figure clearer. He's
at home here, among the dead. He belongs here. Verdun
and Stalingrad and Guernica and Gettysburg. The sadist in
the trench at your side. Cutting quickly now. Montage: piles
of bodies—the plague—the Inquisition—the atomic bomb—
razor wire—napalm. Close-ups. Bottles, pills, Thalidomide,
Hindley and Brady, heroin cut with rat poison. The bin,
filled with body parts after the bus accident. The chalk
outline on the pavement, the suicide and the autopsy and
the draining blue cadaver on the metal slab. That straitjacket. That filthy straitjacket that hurts my shoulders, and
the light bulb with the mesh around it and the rubber mouth
guard. Cue the whispering effect on the soundtrack: "Better
off dead, that one, sitting in his own shit and vomit." . . .
Alone in the dark . . .

Don't make me do this . . .

He is near tears.

And the injections. And the pills. Don't help. Because
everywhere I look it's all witches and witchfinders . . . And
they are so terrible . . . I'm afraid to open my eyes. Because
they'll be there. They will.

He has lost himself in darkness. But his words and his intimate vulnerability have affected **Vincent**.

Vincent   "Sara Lowes, you have been accused this day of consorting with your master, the Devil. Confess your sins or you will suffer the pains of the damned."

Reeves *open his eyes, looks at him.*

The lines are quiet, true, and chilling.

Reeves   "I am no witch, Matthew Hopkins."

Vincent   "Master Stearne will soon prove it otherwise, as legal writ and precedent dictates. Take her . . . And may God have mercy on your poor soul."

Beat.

The moment of creation has touched **Vincent**, *as has* **Reeves'** *obvious psychological damage and painful history.*

Vincent *steps away from* **Reeves**, *pours himself another glass of wine, and thinks as . . .*

Tippi *turns to* **Hitch**, *with a bit of his own bland provocation*:

Tippi   I know you tried to get Grace Kelly.

Hitch   Excuse me?

Tippi   I know you tried to get Grace Kelly.

Hitch   . . . I'm not precisely sure what you mean.

Tippi   Are you not?

Hitch   Did I succeed?

Tippi   If you did I wouldn't be here, would I?

Hitch   No I suppose not.

Tippi *wanders past* **Vincent**—*takes the glass of wine from where he has momentarily set it down*—*and continues.*

Tippi   I mean to play Marnie.

Hitch   I see!

Tippi   What did you think I meant, Hitch?

She stops and looks at him with studied neutrality.

He doesn't answer, watches her a little warily, as . . .

Reeves That was wonderful, Vincent. You changed a line, by the way. You said, "May God have mercy on your *poor* soul." You added the "poor."

Vincent Did I?

Reeves Mmm . . . But you were honest, that's all that counts . . . Isn't that why we do it? Don't we owe ourselves some honesty? Don't we owe that to the audience?

Vincent Michael, we make movies, they're all lies.

Reeves Then they should be honest lies.

Tippi *continues moving around the room . . .*

Tippi You went to Monaco and begged her, didn't you? Read through the script with her. Acted it out. Grace was going to do it, I hear, but her husband said no. "Not befitting the dignity of a princess." . . . I'll say . . . Shame she missed all the late-night dinners. I'm sure she loves consommé and petites quenelles, followed by poached eggs in Chartreuse sauce.

Hitch My unique relationship with Her Serene Highness is my business, Miss Hedren.

Tippi Oh, assuredly. And I guess I'm the happy beneficiary of her decision. I got to play Marnie. What did she get? Aside from running a country.

Hitch Would you change places with her?

Tippi Please. I'm just a simple girl from Minnesota.

Hitch There's nothing simple about you, Miss Hedren.

Tippi You might do well to remember that.

Hitch Yes?

Tippi I'm not so serene.

There's steel in the words. A threat? A promise? He's not sure.

She slowly takes a sip of wine. Gazing at him.

Hitch *makes a tactical retreat . . . He moves away to prepare a cigar, which he never actually lights. But he uses the minutiae of the task to consider his next moves as . . .*

Reeves   Look, I know we disagree on a lot. But I'm only trying to do something with a little *substance.* I know the studio only sees the movie as another exploitation film, another bucket of blood, second cheapie to fill a double feature bill, but it's not, *not to me.*

He goes to a table, finds a telegram.

Reeves   I got this yesterday, from AIP in Hollywood, our illustrious studio. I will quote in full . . . "Saw rushes of pub scene. Want girl's tits naked and blood on tits." . . . So that's it . . . "Blood on tits." . . . And you wonder why my hands shake.

Vincent   So it comes as a surprise that moviemaking is ever so slightly touched with venality? Grow up, Michael. This is our business.

Reeves   *Not mine.*

Vincent   Oh, you're so pure?

Reeves (*tosses the telegram away*)   Purer than those fuckers.

Vincent   You take the money, you play the game.

Reeves *moves away angrily, tension building.*

Reeves   All right, enough.

Vincent   And don't think you're better than anyone else . . . Long time ago I learned this about Hollywood . . . if you sit at the table, don't spit at the other diners.

Reeves   Forgive me for having some *aspiration.*

Vincent   You want to make independent student movies your whole life, go ahead, baby, aspire away. But if you want real cameras, and real lights, and real film stock, and real distribution, and the occasional real ham actor, it costs money. And the money ain't yours.

Reeves   Look, I don't need a lecture from *you*. I know how it works.

Vincent   If you did your hands wouldn't shake.

Reeves   Sorry if I *care* about my work! Sorry if it means something to me!

Vincent   You care too much.

Reeves   How dare you tell me not to care about my work! You're nothing but a fucking *has-been*! Who are you to lecture me?!

Vincent   I've made seventy-five movies, young man! How many have you made?

Reeves   Two *good* ones!

Vincent   That's debatable.

Reeves   Fantastic! I'm going to argue film theory with Egghead.

Vincent   With someone who has spent his *entire life in the service of this art*!

Reeves   *Art?!* You should choke on the word.

Vincent   Don't you dare!

Reeves   Corporate art for Sears-Roebuck, that's you all over.

Vincent   You arrogant little prick.

Reeves   You gave up the right to lecture me when you stopped caring about your work. When you stopped acting and started playing yourself: that jolly/macabre persona you've created to hide your own *hollowness*!—It was when you started doing those Edger Allan Poe films. Maybe we should just turn *Witchfinder General* into another fucking Poe movie?! *Then maybe you wouldn't ruin it with your swishy queer bullshit!*

Vincent   *Michael, this is another fucking Poe movie!*

He's sorry the minute the words are out of this mouth.

Reeves   What are you talking about?

Vincent   I'm tired and a teeny-weeny bit drunk, as are you. That red was repellent by the way.

He goes to get his hat and overcoat.

Reeves   Wait. What do you mean "this is another fucking Poe movie"?

*He takes **Vincent**'s overcoat, won't give it to him.*

Vincent   Give me that.

Reeves   Vincent . . . What are you talking about?

Beat.

Vincent   You want to see the face in the mirror first thing in the morning?

Reeves   What do you mean?

Vincent   You'll want the rouge, trust me.

Reeves   I want the truth.

Vincent   You don't really.

*Beat. **Reeves** looks at him. Waits.*

Vincent   They didn't want you to know . . . In America they're going to release *Witchfinder* as another one of the Poe series. After they've re-edited it of course.

Reeves (*stunned*)   What?

Vincent   They're going to put a new title on it, from one of the poems . . . *The Conqueror Worm.*

Reeves   *Re-edit it?*

Vincent   Yes.

Reeves   They can't.

Vincent   Oh Michael. It's their money. They own it. They can do anything they want.

Reeves *clutches* **Vincent***'s overcoat to him, upset. He retreats to a quiet corner and sits.*

Beat.

Vincent   It's in the left pocket.

Reeves *pulls a compact from the pocket of* **Vincent***'s coat, looks at it.*

Vincent   Max Factor number 17. "Egyptian Gold." Just a bit under the eyes does wonders.

Tippi *simultaneously removes her compact and freshens her makeup.*

Hitch   A compulsion, I told you.

Reeves   It won't help.

Tippi   It'll help.

Vincent   Makes everything a bit prettier.

Tippi   Makes me who you want me to be, doesn't it?

Hitch   You're pretty enough.

Tippi   Pretty enough for what?

Reeves   It'll take more than makeup on a corpse.

Hitch   Pretty enough to go to work. We must rehearse, my dear.

Hitch *moves to the living room area, gets a script.*

Tippi *wanders, looking over the cottage.*

Vincent *nicely brings* **Reeves** *a glass of wine and then wanders, looking over the cottage, passing by* **Tippi** *as she wanders.*

Tippi   This place is bizarre . . . Did I ever mention that? How strange it is?

Hitch   My bungalow?

Tippi   It's an English cottage in the middle of the Universal lot. Doesn't that seem strange?

Vincent   I like your cottage, very rustic it is.

Hitch   Why should it seem strange?

Tippi   We're in California.

Reeves   Studio found the place. Old-fashioned I think.

Hitch   I enjoy old things. Like a Hogarth etching a bit. The Staffordshire dogs especially.

Reeves   I like the china dogs I suppose.

Tippi (*picking up one of the china Staffordshire dogs*)   Pretty.

Vincent (*picking up one of the Staffordshire dogs*)   Imitations.

Hitch   They're not real of course. It's trickery. But isn't everything?

Tippi *and* **Reeves** (*simultaneously*)   Still pretty.

Vincent   Made in China.

Reeves   There are more of them in the bedroom.

Hitch   I have real ones at home. Deployed around my bedroom like a small audience of canine admirers.

Reeves   They're probably fake too.

Tippi   Got to have an audience, don't you?

Hitch   Or admirers.

Reeves   They're really going to re-edit my film?

Vincent   You're twenty-four, Michael. They don't trust you.

Tippi   Who are we without our audience, right?

Reeves   Another bloody Poe film? That's what it's going to be?

Vincent   Yes.

Reeves   Jesus.

He sinks into his chair, depressed. **Vincent** *watches him, sits, concerned.*

Tippi *stops wandering.*

Tippi   It's . . . disorienting. Being in an English country cottage in California. Like you're in two places simultaneously.

Hitch   When I took possession it was decorated in what can only be described as Malibu Moderne: an excess of pillows and wicker. *Wicker*, Miss Hedren! . . . It was like asparagus without the Hollandaise . . . tasteless.

Tippi   At least it looked like what it was. It was honest.

Hitch   Honesty in the motion picture business is highly overrated, if not oxymoronic . . . As Ernst Lubitsch once said: "I've been to Paris France and I've been to Paris Paramount. Paramount is better."

Tippi   But why an English cottage? You could have designed it to look like anyplace. Is that where you were happiest, back in England?

Hitch   Happiness is not a feature of the English character; we are too *apprehensive* . . . No, I was not happy there.

Tippi   Where then?

Hitch *thinks.*

Hitch   Wasco, California.

She looks at him. He enjoys her bewilderment.

Specifically, the Garces Highway near Wasco, north of Bakersfield. It's where we filmed the crop-duster sequence in *North by Northwest* . . . Standing on that crossroads you could see in all directions to the horizon. There was nothing. No shadows . . . Only *stasis*.

He smiles to her.

That is happiness.

Tippi   Mmm . . . I didn't mean to criticize your bungalow. I always liked the painting.

Hitch   J. M. W. Turner.

Tippi   I know . . . I looked it up at the library after the first time I was here. I didn't want to sound stupid if you ever mentioned it . . . The only thing models care about is not sounding stupid. Pretty shallow I guess, trying so hard to have "substance."

Hitch   But you do.

Tippi   Hmm . . . But would I be here tonight if I didn't look like I do? . . . You don't have to answer that. Men have been answering that since I was fourteen.

Beat.

Hitch   My dear, you are transparent before my camera. Every inch of your face, even that minuscule scar on your left eyebrow, the imperfection that makes it all the more poignant. What comes from inside the eyes is what matters . . . the close-up, shooting slightly down, with a key light just catching the lashes . . . Everything that is true emerges from the eyes, you cannot act it . . . This is why Kim Novak will never be truly beautiful on screen, and you will be always.

Tippi   So long as I stay on the island with Mary Rose, where age doesn't matter.

Hitch   Some women age beautifully. It's all in the bone structure and the complexion.

She switches off a lamp as she passes.

Tippi   And the lighting.

Hitch   Grace Kelly. Ingrid Bergman. I'm drawn to the eternal lovelies.

Tippi   Not that it matters. Once you film them, they never change. Like zombies.

Hitch   What a thing to say.

Tippi   Movie stars, zombies, little china dogs. Permanent.

Hitch   That's the glory of it.

Tippi   But it's not real.

Hitch   It's real to me.

Tippi   You need to get out of the movie theater. Go to a Sears-Roebuck sometime. Walk around the aisles. That's reality.

Hitch   Why would I do that?

Tippi   To meet your audience if nothing else. Those for whom you do it.

Hitch   I do it for myself. The audience is no more than the mob in the dark, munching their popcorn, bovine-like.

Tippi   You hate them.

Hitch   Not precisely.

Tippi   What then?

Hitch   I fear them.

Tippi   Why?

Hitch   What if they look away? What if they figure out the magician's trick? What power do I have then? The years of

planning, the months of shooting, the tedium, the
inspiration, the editing, the scoring, finding the film, letting
it speak to me. All for naught if they look away. One glance
to the side. Drop a bit of popcorn and look for it. And I have
lost all power.

Tippi   You have to have power?

Hitch   Don't you?

Tippi   I'm an actress. What power do I have, Hitch?

She looks at him evenly, giving nothing away.

A beat.

He clears his throat.

Hitch   You are obfuscating, little nightingale. Let us
rehearse.

Tippi   Do we have to?

Hitch   We don't want to be unprepared when the moment
comes.

She steels herself.

*She knows the lines by heart. He opens a script and begins to set the
scene:*

Hitch   We start on Sean in the stateroom. You've had the
fight scene from last week, so you've already gone into the
bedroom cabin and closed the door. You're getting ready for
bed: all those mysterious rituals he's never seen . . . But back
in the stateroom he looks at the door, his frustration and
anger building, his erotic drive overwhelming, cut to the
door, cut to him, cut to his face, cut to mid-shot: he gets up
and strides across the room and flings open the door!—You
turn! Dropping your dressing gown.

*She does so, mimes dropping her dressing gown, stays in the moment
throughout:*

You're only in your negligee now. You look at him.

Tippi   Am I surprised?

Hitch   No. You knew this night was coming.

Tippi   Do I scream?

Hitch   Not yet.

Tippi   Why not?

Hitch   It would do no good. There is no rescue. And you love him.

Tippi   I don't love him.

Hitch   You need him. You need him to save you.

Tippi   I don't.

Hitch   To save you from all the men, all the predators since you're fourteen. To save you from your own mediocrity . . . to make you immortal. Still mid-shot. He steps boldly into the room . . . "Marnie, I won't stay out tonight!"

Tippi   "Mark, if you love me you'll let me go. I don't want to be here. How long are you going to keep me trapped?"

Hitch   "Yes, I've caught you. You're a fine and rare animal, and I'm not letting go . . . Someone has to take care of you."

Tippi   "There's no place for you in my life."

Hitch   "We'll make a place. This night has been coming since I first saw you, Marnie, since the moment everything else in my life lost meaning."

Tippi   Wait, that's new.

Hitch   I penciled it in this morning. Your next line's the same.

Tippi   What's the new line?

Hitch   'This night has been coming since I first saw you, Marnie, since the moment everything else in my life lost meaning.'

Tippi   . . . Is that true?

Hitch   Yes.

Tippi   Everything in his life lost meaning? Everything that ever happened before he met her just . . . doesn't matter? Is that true?

Hitch   Everything.

Tippi   God, that's awful. It's so absolute. How can he put that responsibility onto her?

Hitch   He has no choice.

Tippi (*firm*)   There's always a choice.

Hitch   Not for him.

Tippi   So the subtext is his lonely life up to now.

Hitch   Oh, *subtext* is it? Been reading our Stanislavski have we?

Tippi   Don't do that. I'm trying to understand you.

Hitch   Him.

Tippi   Right now you're him.

Hitch   I can't speak to his subtext. I don't see him like an actor does, but as a director.

Tippi   Please. You're the best actor I ever met.

Hitch   The thoughts behind his lines you mean?

Tippi   Underneath them. What's unspoken?

Beat as he thinks about it.

Hitch   Mark has lived a life of comfort. He's earned it through hard work and charm and straight white teeth. But there's something missing. There's a hollowness he hears reverberating at night.

Tippi   And how does he express that to her? What are the words he wants to say?

Hitch   Those in the script.

She keeps pressing:

Tippi   No. Those are the words he's given to say, a ruse; polite and grammatical, *written*. What does he want to *scream*?

Hitch   Does he want to scream?

Tippi   What man doesn't?

Hitch   I don't.

Tippi   She could only love a man who was willing to scream.

Hitch   Then she is disturbed.

Tippi   You ought to know, you created her.

Hitch   Well—

Tippi   She's passionate and willful. She can't be won by clean white teeth; she's had a lifetime of them. She wants him to scream.

Hitch   He's too civilized to scream.

Tippi   Then he doesn't deserve to be in the scene with her. She's an animal, and she needs another animal.

Hitch   That's simply not him.

Tippi   Isn't it?

Beat . . . **Hitch** *is uncomfortable. He reorients himself, taking control again.*

Hitch   From the top if you please. Take your time . . . You're getting ready for bed . . . He walks into the cabin . . .

She again mimes dropping her dressing gown, again stays in the moment throughout:

Hitch   "Marnie, I won't stay out tonight!"

Tippi   "Mark, if you love me you'll let me go. I don't want to be here. How long are you going to keep me trapped?"

Hitch   "Yes, I've caught you. You're a fine and rare animal, and I'm not letting go . . . Someone has to take care of you."

Tippi   "There's no place for you in my life."

Hitch   "We'll make a place. This night has been coming since I first saw you, Marnie, since the moment everything else in my life lost meaning."

Tippi   "I'm tired; we'll talk about it tomorrow. Get out."

Hitch   "Well, if you're tired you should go to bed . . . We should both go to bed."

Tippi (*screams*)   "NO!"

Hitch   He's shocked by the ferocity of the scream. He looks at you. Close-up. Mid-shot . . . (**Hitch** *mimes.*) . . . But he suddenly reaches out—rips off your negligee! It falls. You're naked!

She stands there . . . frozen . . . eyes full of trauma.

You're naked before him. Everything he's dreamed about . . . That perfection he's created in his head, that fresh skin he's gazed at for so long . . . Yet he feels guilty too. He loathes himself. He's done something ugly; he's ugly. He knows you don't love him . . . "I'm sorry, Marnie" . . . He steps in—mid-shot—and puts his dressing gown over your bare shoulders . . .

He puts his suit jacket over her shoulders. It's intimate. Whispers now . . .

Close-up . . . Their faces fill the screen . . .

She doesn't move, stares forward.

As in the scene from Marnie, **Hitch** *caresses her hair . . . her face
. . . closer . . . his lips moving gently over her face . . . and finally
finding her lips.*

A long kiss.

Her expression doesn't change.

He steps back.

He doesn't know what to do.

*Then he knows. He becomes a director again . . . He slowly raises his
hands . . . He frames her face coldly, a director mechanically lining
up a close-up.*

Hitch   We stay on her face as he eases her back . . . onto the
bed . . . as he sticks it in her . . . We never leave her face, big
close-up . . . Her expression . . . Ah . . . Then we pan over to
the porthole . . . we see the moonlight on the ocean, the
music swells romantically . . .

Beat.

She breaks the scene.

*She discards his coat on a chair and moves away, gathering her
thoughts and her strength.*

*His bland, professional demeanor doesn't change through the
following:*

Hitch   We'll use a crane to get you on the bed, rather like
Martin Balsam on the stairs in *Psycho,* but I didn't like that
rear projection so we'll do it practical. You'll just lie there
and the crane will lower you down, staying tight on your
face. It'll be a touch claustrophobic I daresay with the
camera rig on top of you, you should take off your clothes
now and go into the bedroom. Remembering always that
you're under personal contract and it is imperative not to
displease your employer or perhaps he'll lose interest in
your career, which would be a shame given all the time we've
put into you, myself and the studio. I'm sure it would get

around town, how difficult you are. I'm not sure who else
would hire you. And as any true friend will tell you, at your
age modeling work will be hard to come by and that handy
compact less effective, so taking care of your daughter might
prove onerous. The bedroom's in there. You can leave the
gloves on if you like, though I don't mind, your choice.

Beat.

*She turns, gets her purse, and walks to the hallway to the outside, as
if to leave the bungalow for good . . .*

But then she stops . . . Suspends . . .

Beat . . .

She turns . . .

She walks across the room to the doorway into the bedroom . . .

But she stops again . . . Waits . . .

*She finally turns and walks back to the dining table. She sits,
thinking deeply.*

Hitch *just stands there, gazing at her . . . Awaiting her response.*

As **Reeves** *rises, deep in thought, trying to work something out.*

He moves downstage, switching on the lamp that **Tippi** *had
previously turned off. He passes by* **Hitch**.

*The two worlds are fully invading each other now, sharing the same
space more; the characters are like ghosts in each other's stories.*

Reeves   Do you know Hitchcock?

Vincent   What?

Reeves   Hitchcock's work.

Vincent   Yes.

Reeves   There's a moment in *Marnie* . . . Not a seminal
work surely. I mean, it's not Pasolini, no one teaches it in
film studies . . . But there's a moment . . . beyond exultation.

Mid-way through the film Sean Connery confronts Tippi
Hedren on a ship. He rips off her nightgown and she stands
there naked in front of him. And the look in her eyes . . .
Utterly vulnerable; raw and traumatized and proud
simultaneously . . . It might be the finest piece of film acting
I've ever seen . . .

Vincent *isn't sure where he's going.*

Reeves   Now Tippi Hedren isn't necessarily the world's
greatest actress . . . *So how did she do it?* . . . How did they do it
together? . . . By all accounts they had a complicated
relationship, art and Eros all mixed up. But tonight I think
. . . I think maybe that was it. That's how they did it. As
horrible and humiliating as it was, that's how they made a
moment of grace. I wonder if it was worth it for them.

He looks at **Vincent**.

Reeves   All my life I've been looking for someone to make
me want to leave the darkened cinema.

Beat.

*He slowly pulls off his shirt . . . Then steps out of his loafers and
removes most or all of his clothes . . . He stands before* **Vincent**.

*He's totally available, totally vulnerable; raw and traumatized and
proud simultaneously.*

Reeves   Please, don't leave.

He is in tears now.

Vincent *slowly walks to him, finding the vulnerability almost
unbearably poignant.*

He touches **Reeves**' *face gently, wipes away his tears.*

Then **Vincent** *steps away . . . He gets his overcoat, brings it to*
Reeves *and very gently puts it around his shoulders.*

As **Hitch** *moves to another position, passing by* **Vincent**, *re-
orienting himself to* **Tippi**, *watching her.*

Hitch   Did you not understand your character's motivation, Miss Hedren?

She looks at him as **Vincent** *finally speaks*:

Vincent   Despite that lifetime in darkened cinemas, you have more perception than you think . . . You were on the money about one thing . . . my career's pretty much over. I don't think the studio's going to pick up my contract. Hell, I can't blame them . . . movies are all drugs and motorcycles and rock music nowadays. Who needs a camp old grand dame like me? What was it you said? "Has-been." Has. Been. Playing to an empty house. It happens to all show-folk in the end. So you dye your temples to start. Then the rest. Then you steal bits of your wife's makeup. Then you buy your own. Then you have the littlest facelift. You embarrass yourself at the gymnasium so the body won't be so repulsive to young eyes. What a foolish old man you've become. When did that happen? . . . What do I do? What's my next line?

He is lost in thought.

Hitch   I believe you have a line, my dear. Shall I prompt you again?

Reeves *gets another glass of wine . . . Then he sits at the dining table right next to* **Tippi**.

Vincent *gets his hat, prepares to leave the room.*

Vincent   You can keep the coat. Goodbye and good luck, my friend.

Reeves   Please. Don't go. Look, I know it's hard, feeling all this. But isn't it better to risk it? To feel something . . . Shouldn't we try for that as long as we're alive?

Vincent   The way I feel tonight, kid, that won't be very long.

Reeves   Oh, you're immortal. You're a movie star. You'll outlive us all. Especially me.

Vincent   How can you say that?

Reeves *speaks with simple and unsentimental truth*:

Reeves   I can't survive the art form I've chosen . . . "Blood on tits" . . . It'll be the pills or the needle or the madhouse again, then the mortician and the Max Factor number 17. Give me a pad, I'll storyboard it.

Vincent   You are so young. Think of the stories you have yet to tell.

Reeves   I just want to tell this one . . . Please . . . Don't leave the film. It's all I have. Let's tell this story like it matters, Vincent, you and me.

Vincent *is torn. Thinking.*

Tippi *takes the glass of wine from the table before* **Reeves** *and takes a sip.*

She's ready.

Tippi   Three years I've been waiting for this moment, wondering how I would react . . . It's not just me. Everyone knows it's been coming. Everyone on the set knows, not that I think you care. I asked for help, you know. I did. I went to the A.D. and then I went to the studio and even the front office. I went to my agent and my manager. I begged them to do something. I begged everyone to help, to talk to you, to put an end to this. They wouldn't. Make him happy, they said. Think of your career. He's Alfred Hitchcock. You're just The Girl.

And The Girl is to be looked at, isn't she? That's what she's for. So you watch me. All day long you watch me on the set. You watch me through the lens. You watch me in the dailies. You watch me in editing. You possess my face and manipulate it any way you want. Open your mouth. Not so much. Moisten your lips. Raise your chin. Find your light. Tilt to the left. Hold. Don't move. Don't breathe. Don't think. Close-up. It's not even my face anymore, is it? That little scar on my left eyebrow, is it still there?

Hitch *opens his mouth to speak. She silences him—*

Tippi   Wait. It's not your line. Before you say anything, I have a question . . . *What happens if I say yes?* That's what you want. And sooner or later you always get what you want, right?

Hitch *doesn't answer. She rivets him.*

Tippi   *"What if?"* . . . We become lovers, right in there, five minutes from now. Naturally you can't stay with Alma after we're together, that would be insulting to us both. So you leave your wife of, what is it, near on forty years. Then what happens? What's the film in your head? . . . Fade up: You walk out on Alma and life goes on happily, like a scene from a movie where you can cut out all the ugly things you don't want anyone to see, all the shots where the boom's in the frame, all the scenes of poor old Alma discarded on the editing-room floor . . . Cut to: Bright sunny day with no shadows. You sell the house in Bel Air and we find somewhere to live together: our little English cottage in sun-kissed Santa Monica where we'll cook dinners and make great movies and walk on the beach and you can frame the sunset fade-out: pan over to see the moonlight on the ocean, the music swells romantically . . . Cut to: Exterior. Night. Inevitably we start going out in public, like couples do. We walk the red carpet together: lots of flashing cameras and gossip columnists scribbling notes. You touch the small of my back, very gently controlling me, demonstrating your ownership, turning me in unison, smiling, smiling. Everyone you know is laughing behind your back. You hear them don't you? Cue the whispering effect on the soundtrack: "Poor Hitch and his piece of ass: threw it all away for her. Half his age and she's not even that pretty. No Grace Kelly. There was a piece of ass. What a foolish old man he's become. Tell you, his last movie wasn't so great either. It's her. She's not a very good actress, is she?" Which I know, by the way. What's the word you used? "Mediocre" . . . I know what I am. But do you know what you are . . .?

She gradually circles closer, moving in for the kill.

Do you want to know? . . . Do you want to know what your "muse" thinks? What's inside that jolly/macabre persona you've created to hide your own hollowness? . . . You're the ugly boy with Cary Grant inside, clawing to get out. You're so desperate to prove to yourself you're not Claude Rains, or Robert Walker, or Mrs. Danvers, or Norman Bates, you want to scream it: I'm Cary Grant goddamn it, I'm Jimmy Stewart, I'm Gregory Peck. I'm handsome. I'm thin. I'm young. I'm brave. I'm wise. I'm good. *I'm the hero* . . . God, I would strip off my clothes and let you take me right now if it would make you believe that for five minutes. But it won't . . . Because you *know* who you are, Hitch . . . Don't worry, they're always the juiciest parts in your movies.

She slowly moves toward him.

And you don't fool me with this vulgar approach, this ridiculous sexual threat: "I'll ruin your career if you don't get in there and fuck me." Nonsense. You don't want a whore, you could have plenty of them, one call from your secretary to Lew Wasserman and you could have girls lined up to Lankershim Boulevard. No, you don't want a whore, you want a *co-star*; someone to make you feel young and alive and handsome all the way until the credits roll. And what if this is your very last chance *to finally get your blonde*? . . . You can talk about fucking as much as you want, but your eyes tell the truth: close-up, shooting slightly down, with a key light just catching the lashes. Everything that is true emerges from the eyes, you can't act it . . . *You're in love* . . . Why don't you admit it? Just be honest. Say the words. Rehearse the scene. Be the hero.

Hitch *turns . . . starts to walk out.*

Tippi   *Stop.*

He does.

I didn't say "cut" . . . Turn back to me . . . (*He starts to turn.*)
. . . other way . . . (*He turns in the other direction, faces her.*) . . .
Stop. Raise your chin. Find your light.

She walks right up to him.

Tippi   Mr. Hitchcock, The Girl says no.

Beat.

Vincent   . . . What was the line?

Reeves   What?

Vincent   Your favorite movie line. What was it?

Reeves   Oh . . . "You want to know something? I don't
think Mozart's going to help at all."

Hitch *clears his throat and speaks*:

Hitch   Miss Hedren . . . It is not unknown in my profession
for there to be . . . *misunderstandings* . . . It is not unknown for
leading performers to mistake a director's professional
ministrations for something closer to the personal. I'm sorry
you have misinterpreted my actions as any particular
interest in you whatsoever.

She looks at him, saddened by his response.

Vincent   What's it from?

Reeves   *Vertigo*. It's Barbara Bel Geddes, talking to the
doctor after Jimmy Stewart's breakdown.

Hitch   You are a tool to me. You do not exist beyond the
soundstage. You do not exist outside of the frame. You do
not exist after the credits rolls. There is no "what if?" . . . You
are the MacGuffin.

Reeves   The doctor is playing a record of Mozart, hoping to
cure Jimmy Stewart of his heartbreak after Kim Novak dies.
And she says, "You want to know something? I don't think
Mozart's going to help at all." . . . I think what she means is
when you care about something deeply there's nothing to be

done. There's no cure . . . You just have to keep on caring and hope you survive.

Tippi   Keep on caring and hope you survive . . .

Hitch   What was that?

Tippi   What I tell my daughter. About this life.

She gathers her things to go, putting on her green scarf again, crossing by . . .

Vincent *is thinking, deciding . . .*

Reeves *watches him.*

Tippi *is crossing to leave when—*

Hitch *suddenly stands quickly!*

Tippi *stops; looks at him.*

Is he going to speak? Is he going to scream?

Suspense.

Vincent   . . . Can you do me a favor?

Reeves   What?

Vincent   On the set tomorrow – and yes, I will be there – wear those tight striped pants . . . Now where's that fucking script!

He puts on his glasses and goes to get the script as **Reeves** *drops his head, overcome with relief.*

Hitch *lowers his eyes, speaks quietly:*

Hitch   Miss Hedren . . . Tippi . . . Tippi . . .

Beat . . .

She waits . . .

He finally looks up at her . . .

Hitch   I have already informed you that scarf is maladroit with that ensemble.

Beat.

Tippi *slowly raises her hands and frames* **Hitch** *in the shot, as he has done to her countless times over the years, capturing him.*

Tippi   Cut. Print. That's a wrap.

Blackout.

The End.

9 781350 471641